The Co-Parenting Chronicles
Shared Parenting Strategies

Table of Contents

1. Introduction 1

2. The Journey of Co-Parenting: An Introduction 2

   2.1. The Landscape of Shared Parenting 2

   2.2. The Road Map: Constructive Co-Operation 2

   2.3. The Passengers: The Children 3

   2.4. The Roadblocks: Emotions and Communication 3

   2.5. Toolkit for the Journey: Self-Care, Patience, and Persistence . . 4

   2.6. The Destination: Shared Parenting Confidence 4

3. Legal Boundaries in Shared Parenting 6

   3.1. Understanding Shared Parenting Laws 6

   3.2. Custody Types and their Legal Implications 6

   3.3. The Importance of Parenting Plans 7

   3.4. Legal Recourses in Conflicts 8

   3.5. Navigating Child Support Legally 8

4. Understanding Emotions: Yours and Your Child's 10

   4.1. Identifying Your Emotions 10

   4.2. Understanding Your Emotions 11

   4.3. Managing Your Emotions 11

   4.4. Emotion Coaching Your Child 11

   4.5. Emotion Coaching in Co-Parenting 12

5. Creating Effective Communication Channels 13

   5.1. The Elements of Constructive Communication 13

   5.2. Structured and Consistent Communication Formats 13

   5.3. Using Technology to Your Advantage 14

   5.4. Focusing on the Issues, Not the Person 14

   5.5. Framing your Communication 14

   5.6. Active Listening 15

   5.7. The Importance of Clarity and Transparency 15

5.8. Patience and Persistence ... 15

6. Scheduling Strategies: Streamlining Lives ... 17

6.1. Mastering the Art of Flexible Schedules ... 17

6.2. Emphasizing Consistency ... 17

6.3. The Digital Advantage: Leveraging Technology ... 18

6.4. Holidays, Vacations, and Special Occasions ... 18

6.5. Time for Transitions ... 19

6.6. Importance of Communication ... 19

7. Impact of Co-parenting on Children: A Psychological View ... 21

7.1. The Influence on Overall Development ... 21

7.2. Emotional Stability in Children ... 21

7.3. Facilitating Resilience ... 22

7.4. Impact on Self-Esteem and Identity ... 22

7.5. Lessons on Relationships and Respect ... 23

8. Financial Aspects in Co-Parenting ... 24

8.1. Creating a Shared Budget ... 24

8.2. Implementing the Shared Budget ... 24

8.3. Child Support ... 25

8.4. College Savings ... 25

8.5. Maintaining Financial Stability ... 26

8.6. Navigating Financial dispute ... 26

9. Maintaining Consistent Parenting Styles ... 27

9.1. Understanding Parenting Styles ... 27

9.2. Creating a Unified Parenting Plan ... 28

9.3. Communication is Key ... 28

9.4. Addressing Differences and Disagreements ... 29

9.5. Managing Transitions Between Households ... 29

10. Dealing with Conflict: Mature Approaches ... 31

10.1. Building a Collaborative Mindset ... 31

10.2. Communicating Effectively ... 31

10.3. Cultivating Empathy 32

10.4. Fostering Mutual Respect 32

10.5. Developing a Conflict Resolution Strategy 32

10.6. Engaging in Mediation 32

10.7. Attending to Your Own Emotional Health 33

11. Co-Parenting Success Stories: Lessons from Real Life 34

11.1. From Enemies to Allies 34

11.2. Overcoming Business of Life 34

11.3. Accepting New Challenges 35

11.4. Understanding Children's Needs 35

11.5. The Power of Consistency 36

Chapter 1. Introduction

Welcome to a fresh perspective on navigating shared parenting! Our Special Report, "The Co-Parenting Chronicles: Shared Parenting Strategies," unravels the complexities of juggling schedules, managing emotions, and fostering positive growth for your children in a co-parenting scenario. This report empowers you with practical tips, genuine insights, and expert advice, making the co-parenting journey smoother and more fulfilling. It's not just a guide, it serves as your friendly partner in enabling harmonious shared parenting. If you've ever felt daunted by the challenges of co-parenting, let this cheerful and inspiring report light your way towards constructive cooperation and mutual respect. Secure your copy today and step into a new era of shared parenting confidence!

Chapter 2. The Journey of Co-Parenting: An Introduction

Co-parenting is a labyrinth of complex emotions, responsibilities, and situations. Navigating through this maze might appear daunting at first glance, but understanding the journey can help make the process smoother and more fulfilling. This introduction aims to paint an insightful picture of the co-parenting journey, addressing its inherent complexities and offering a map for constructive co-operation and mutual respect.

2.1. The Landscape of Shared Parenting

Shared parenting doesn't happen in a vacuum. It's played out within a landscape marked by past experiences, existing situations, and future aspirations. The emotions of the involved parties - parents and children alike - can shape the nature of shared parenting to great extents. Understanding the landscape helps set expectations, allowing all involved parties to prepare and adapt to the realities of shared parenting.

Shared parenting is a journey that begins as soon as you and your ex-partner decide to part ways. This decision marks the beginning of a unique journey, the end of which is not a destination, but rather an ongoing process of growth, communication, and understanding.

2.2. The Road Map: Constructive Co-Operation

Co-parenting is not a path etched in stone - it's flexible and fluid, accommodating the evolving needs and dynamics of the family. Key to this journey is co-operation. And contrary to popular belief, this doesn't always mean complete agreement between the parents on all issues. More pragmatically, it's about respecting set processes and principles in the best interest of the child. It involves creating a parenting plan, defining modes of communication, and setting clear boundaries.

Having a road map makes the journey easier; however, the unpredictability of situations and human emotions can always usher in detours. Therefore, having flexibility is critical. Being adaptable to changes paves the way for mutual understanding and respectful communication.

2.3. The Passengers: The Children

Perhaps the most significant passengers on your co-parenting journey are the children. Their welfare, emotions, and growth remain central to all shared parenting decisions and practices. Children inherently need love, understanding, and security, and the manner in which shared parenting is carried out can greatly influence how they perceive these elements.

Children are adaptable and resilient, yet sensitive. A harmonious co-parenting environment can foster positive growth, while an acrimonious one may lead to negative behavioral patterns. Thus, taking cues from the child's emotions and behavior, and modifying co-parenting strategies accordingly, is crucial.

2.4. The Roadblocks: Emotions and Communication

Roadblocks are inevitable in any journey, and shared parenting is no exception. Two common stumbling blocks are emotions and communication. Emotionally driven decisions can often deviate from the best interest of the child, but recognising and counteracting emotional biases can help keep the journey on track.

Communication is the lifeblood of shared parenting. Poor communication or misunderstanding can become roadblocks. Ensuring clear, open, and respectful communication channels can help eliminate many problems.

2.5. Toolkit for the Journey: Self-Care, Patience, and Persistence

Shared parenting, like any other journey, requires specific tools. The tools in this case are intangible but extraordinarily significant. Self-care is one such vital tool. Taking care of one's mental and emotional wellbeing ensures a healthier co-parenting environment.

Patience and persistence are other critical tools. The process can often be exhausting and might seem unending, but patience can help see out most storms. Persistence, despite the setbacks, ensures co-parenting endures.

2.6. The Destination: Shared Parenting Confidence

There usually is no 'final destination' in the journey of co-parenting, but choosing to see shared parenting confidence as the endpoint can make the journey rewarding and fulfilling. The goal is to foster a mechanism whereby parents and children interact in a healthy, respectful, and mature manner.

This introduction has laid the foundation for understanding the journey of shared parenting, highlighting several key elements such as the landscape of shared parenting, co-operational road-map, the passengers or the children, handling roadblocks like emotions and communication, and ultimately, tools of self-care, patience, and persistence required along the journey.

Chapter 3. Legal Boundaries in Shared Parenting

Navigating the labyrinth of the legal world when it comes to shared parenting can prove challenging, however, with the right guidance and comprehension, parents can successfully manage this domain while providing their children with the best possible environment. Let's dissect the various legal aspects that impact shared parenting, forming an essential bulwark of this co-parenting edifice.

3.1. Understanding Shared Parenting Laws

In the realm of shared parenting, knowledge is power. The laws vary considerably between jurisdictions, so the first step is to understand the provisions and legal stipulations in your specific region. Often, courts aim to allocate parenting rights and duties in a way that aligns with the child's best interests. Some common factors that the court considers include the child's age, emotional bond with parents, parents' physical and mental health, and past parental conduct.

Bear in mind that you, as well as your co-parent, are entitled to legal representation and this is especially important when disagreements arise. Consulting with a qualified family law attorney who is familiar with shared parenting laws can help you understand how these laws apply to your circumstances.

3.2. Custody Types and their Legal Implications

Several different types of custody arrangements can affect your shared parenting setup:

- **Legal Custody:** It refers to the parent's right to make significant decisions about a child's life, including education, healthcare, religion, and overall wellbeing. Often, courts favor awarding joint legal custody, implying that both parents have an equal say in decision-making.

- **Physical Custody:** Pertaining to where the child lives and who cares for them on a day-to-day basis. Joint physical custody does not necessarily mean equal time but rather significant periods of time with both parents.

- **Sole Custody:** Here, one parent has both legal and physical custody. This is generally granted when one parent is deemed unfit due to neglect, abuse or other significant issues.

- **Joint Custody:** Both parents share legal and/or physical custody. This is increasingly becoming a standard where feasible and is seen as embodying the principles of shared parenting.

Remember, legal designations are not, in themselves, parenting plans. Instead, they help set the boundaries of what each parent can expect from the other.

3.3. The Importance of Parenting Plans

A well-structured parenting plan is a non-negotiable tool in shared parenting. It outlines how the co-parents will share and manage the rights and responsibilities of parenting, ranging from physical living arrangements, holiday schedules to matters concerning education, healthcare, and discipline practices.

For a parenting plan to be legally binding, it must be approved by the court. Therefore, once both parents agree upon the contents, it is generally written up (often by a lawyer), signed by both parents, and submitted to the court for approval. Once okayed by the court, it becomes a court order with legal implications, i.e., failure to comply can lead to legal penalties.

3.4. Legal Recourses in Conflicts

Conflicts are an undesirable, though often inevitable, part of shared parenting. Understanding your legal options in such instances becomes critical.

If a co-parent violates the stipulations of a court-approved parenting plan, legal recourse varies across jurisdictions. You may need to file a motion for contempt of court order, which can lead to penalties for the non-compliant parent, remedial services, or a possible modification in the parenting plan.

In case of a stand-off on parenting decisions, the court might have to step in. While the type of decision disputed can dictate the process, it's often best to have steps outlined in your parenting plan for dispute resolution, which may include mediation or, less desirably, court intervention.

3.5. Navigating Child Support Legally

Child support is a significant part of the legal conversation surrounding shared parenting. It is the means to ensure the financial needs of the child are met irrespective of the parents' relationship status. It typically involves payments made by a noncustodial parent to the custodial one and is legally enforceable.

The amount often depends on the parents' respective incomes, the child's needs, and the time each parent spends with the child. Deviation from the stipulated child support obligations can have serious legal repercussions.

Remember, open communication and understanding can

significantly ease the transition into shared parenting. However, where there are bumps in the road, knowledge of the relevant laws and having the right legal support can help keep the best interests of your child front and center.

Chapter 4. Understanding Emotions: Yours and Your Child's

Accepting, embracing, and understanding your emotions and that of your child is a critical capability to foster successful co-parenting. Not only does it assist you in self-care, but it also provides a framework for understanding your child's emotional experience. This chapter begins with an in-depth exploration of these dual emotional journeys, offering insight, guidance, and practical advice along the way.

4.1. Identifying Your Emotions

You're human and, like everyone else, you have a wide spectrum of emotions. Anger, joy, stress, excitement, frustration, contentment... the list goes on. A co-parenting arrangement, existing after the end of a romantic relationship, often brings a flurry of feelings to the forefront. Identifying your emotions is the first step towards understanding them.

Use emotional self-awareness: constantly check in with your feelings. There's a misconception that labeling emotions make them stronger, but the opposite is true. Acknowledging emotions lessens their hold on you, particularly the negative ones. Try to be as specific as possible, moving beyond happy, sad, angry, or stressed, to emotions such as gratitude, disappointment, or contentment.

Record your feelings: keeping a journal can help in monitoring emotional shifts and patterns. It offers you a private space to express your feelings and serves as a mirror for self-reflection.

4.2. Understanding Your Emotions

Having identified your feelings, the next step involves understanding them. Emotions act as messengers carrying information about your current state of being, your needs, your desires, or even your boundaries.

Look beneath the surface: beneath every emotion is a need waiting to be addressed. For instance, continuous frustration might be hinting at deep-seated need for stress management tools, while constant anger might suggest unresolved issues.

Connect the dots: tie your emotions to the circumstances that sparked them. This improves your emotional awareness, helping you predict and cope with them in future similar situations.

4.3. Managing Your Emotions

Managing your emotions requires effort and consistency. Emotions can be overwhelming—especially the negative ones—yet don't push them away. Allow them to flow naturally; suppression can lead to emotional pile-up and eventual explosion.

Practice mindfulness: being present with your feelings without judging or resisting them. Remember, it's okay to feel what you feel.

Seek professional help: if you're having trouble dealing with your emotions, don't hesitate to seek professional help. Therapy can be a useful tool for navigating through emotional difficulties.

4.4. Emotion Coaching Your Child

Understanding your child's emotions means being attuned to their feelings and offering guidance when needed. Validating their emotions assists in building their emotional intelligence.

Active listening: listen to your child, comfort them, and make them feel heard and understood.

Normalize emotions: children should know that all emotions are valid and normalize them. Teach them it's okay to feel sad, angry, or frustrated, and they should never feel ashamed of their feelings.

Teaching emotional skills: equip your child with the skills to identify, understand, and manage their emotions. Storytelling, role-playing, and using creative illustrations can be effective methods.

4.5. Emotion Coaching in Co-Parenting

Your co-parenting dynamic significantly influences your child's emotional wellbeing. Let co-parenting practices reflect an emotionally healthy environment for your child.

Maintain a united front: shelter your child from any co-parenting disputes. Communicate clearly and calmly to ensure consistency between homes.

Model healthy emotions: be an example to your child regarding emotional expression. Demonstrating mature emotional control is a priceless lesson they can carry into adulthood.

In conclusion, understanding emotions—yours and your child's—is a crucial step in the co-parenting journey. By cultivating emotional intelligence, you prepare both yourself and your child for the different chapters that shared parenting might write. It might be challenging, there may be frustrating times, but the rewards speak for themselves in the form of nurturing, self-reliant and emotionally secure children, and a satisfying transition to this new phase of your life.

Chapter 5. Creating Effective Communication Channels

Communication is arguably one of the most critical cornerstones in co-parenting. Flexibility, empathy, and mutual understanding can not be fostered without establishing clear and effective lines of communication. This involves more than just regular conversations; it means designing a comprehensive communication strategy that reduces friction and encourages constructive exchanges. So, how can one put such a strategy in place? This chapter delves into that, advising strategies for creating effective communication channels between co-parents.

5.1. The Elements of Constructive Communication

First things first, let's define what constructive communication looks like in a co-parenting scenario. It's respectful and courteous, with a focus on problem-solving rather than finger-pointing. Key elements of this type of communication include empathy, clarity, consistency, and a friendly tone. Constructive communication also involves active listening, which involves fully understanding the other person's point of view before responding.

5.2. Structured and Consistent Communication Formats

Consistency is key to maintaining clear communication. Having particular formats and mediums for specific discussions can make communication more efficient. For instance, text messages or emails could be used for immediate matters that require quick responses, like schedule changes or health concerns. More complex or open-ended discussions, such as decisions about schooling or talking through disagreements, might be better suited for phone calls or face-to-face meetings, where tone and nuance can be more accurately conveyed.

5.3. Using Technology to Your Advantage

There are several communication tools designed specifically for co-parents that can be utilised. Technology offers options like shared calendars for scheduling, document storage for relevant files, note-sharing capabilities for non-urgent issues, and messaging platforms for day-to-day communication. Such platforms centralize information and can minimise misunderstandings by keeping communication clear and easy to reference.

5.4. Focusing on the Issues, Not the Person

One of the pitfalls co-parents can fall into is allowing their personal feelings towards each other to cloud constructive communication. It's essential to stay objective and focus on the issues at hand, rather than letting the conversation veer into personal gripes. Keep the conversation centered on the child's needs and wellbeing. It's important that personal conflicts do not overshadow the core purpose of the conversation - your children's best interests.

5.5. Framing your Communication

Similar to above, make your communication child-centric. State your observations, feelings, and needs in a clear, concise, and respectful manner. Use "I" statements to express thoughts rather than "you" statements, which can feel accusatory. For example, "I felt worried when Johnny came home late from your house" is a more effective way of communicating than "You never get Johnny home on time".

5.6. Active Listening

Active listening makes the other person feel valued and heard. It encourages open dialogue and helps in understanding and addressing the root cause of any problem. Repeat back what you understand from their messages, ask clarifying questions, and show empathy for their feelings.

5.7. The Importance of Clarity and Transparency

While communicating with your co-parent, spell out specifics. Confusion often results from vague conversations, which can lead to frustrations down the line. Whether you're discussing summer vacation plans or laying out health concerns, be clear and transparent. This can prevent misunderstandings and demonstrate that you value open communication.

5.8. Patience and Persistence

Improvements in communication might not happen quickly. Learning new ways to communicate effectively requires patience and persistence. Don't get discouraged if there are hiccups along the way, and keep open to revising your communication strategy as needed to find what works best for both parties.

In closing, establish respectful and courteous communication, consistent practices, using technology as an aid, focusing on issues, framing communication around the child, active listening, clarity, and transparency. Patience and persistence in implementing these strategies can dramatically improve the co-parenting experience, making it a positive environment for everyone involved.

Chapter 6. Scheduling Strategies: Streamlining Lives

To experience harmonious co-parenting, consider your shared parenting journey akin to running a well-oiled machine. Much like the diverse cogs that underpin such a machine, there are various aspects that need seamless integration. Amongst these, schedules stand as one of the most crucial. They are the blueprint that carves out your day-to-day activities, acting as the backbone of your co-parenting routine. It is, therefore, vital to efficiently streamline your schedules to ensure the smooth functioning of your shared parenting arrangements.

6.1. Mastering the Art of Flexible Schedules

When drafting a co-parenting calendar, one must not lose sight of the virtue of flexibility. Despite being a well-charted plan, schedules should be versatile enough to accommodate sudden changes.

Life, as we know it, is unpredictable. Whether it's an unexpected illness, an impromptu school event or a sudden business meeting, mitigating these scenarios to your schedule without causing unnecessary disruptions becomes an essential part of a proficient co-parenting arrangement. Build buffers into your timelines and have a Plan B ready in case a course correction is required.

6.2. Emphasizing Consistency

While flexibility is key, it shouldn't come at the cost of consistency.

Maintaining a consistent schedule sets a predictable routine for your children, making them feel secure and comfortable.

Understand the importance of regularity in your kid's life, from school days to extracurricular activities, homework timeline, leisure, and bedtime. Emphasize on creating a schedule whose backbone stands on the ground of predictability and constancy. This contributes to their overall well-being and development, and also strengthens their sense of security.

6.3. The Digital Advantage: Leveraging Technology

In today's rapidly digitizing world, technology can significantly simplify scheduling. Numerous applications and digital platforms specialize in co-parenting schedules, complete with reminders, shared access, and real-time updates.

They allow both parents to input, modify, synchronize, and view schedules simultaneously. This reduces potential misunderstandings and enhances transparency. It's also beneficial for children to have access, as it allows them to keep up with their routines without constantly checking with their parents.

6.4. Holidays, Vacations, and Special Occasions

Special days require special attention. Whether it's your child's birthday or holiday seasons like Christmas or Thanksgiving, planning for these in advance can save you a lot of last-minute hassles.

Establish clear communication with your co-parent about who gets to spend time with the children on what holidays, and maintain a rotation system to ensure fairness. Similarly, vacations need advanced planning to balance shared time and make sure that the kids get equal time with both parents.

6.5. Time for Transitions

Transitions are another essential element to consider while drafting your shared parenting schedule. The transition days are not just about the physical shift of the child from one parent's house to another, but also about adjusting to the emotional shift that comes with it.

Ample time should be scheduled for these transitions to help reduce their stress and anxiety. It could be by scheduling transition days on weekends or non-school days to allow children to adjust at their own pace without the pressure of school work.

6.6. Importance of Communication

While all the above strategies can help streamline your shared parenting schedule, the underpinning factor that glues everything together is communication. Keep your co-parent informed about any changes, ensuring you both are on the same page about every decision.

Consider your co-parent as a teammate rather than an opponent. You both are working towards a single goal: the well-being of your children. Maintaining a positive dialog not only helps in efficient schedule management but also sets a good example for the children.

Shared parenting is a journey filled with the complex interplay of emotions, responsibilities, and schedules. Being patient, flexible, and communicative are critical elements in this journey. While meticulously planning schedules is important, do not forget to accommodate for the spontaneous moments that make parenting such a fulfilling experience. Let the schedules not just be plans but become the doorway to forging lasting bonds.

Remember, at the end of the day, the focus should always be on creating nurturing environments that let your children grow and flourish. Let these co-parenting scheduling strategies guide you towards that path.

Chapter 7. Impact of Co-parenting on Children: A Psychological View

Acknowledging the fact that co-parenting can reap significant benefits for children requires a closer examination from a psychological perspective. Not only does co-parenting impact children's immediate circumstances, it also contributes to their future mental and emotional health.

7.1. The Influence on Overall Development

There's no denying that co-parenting leads to increased child development and stability. Given that both parents are involved in the child's life, each parent can contribute to the child's development based on their strengths. For instance, if one parent is more academically inclined, they can support the child's education, while the other parent might excel in cultivating the child's social or creative skills.

Moreover, the child also gets the chance to observe and absorb a diverse range of skills, viewpoints, and methods of problem-solving. This exposure contributes to better cognitive, social, and emotional development, helping the child become a well-rounded individual.

7.2. Emotional Stability in Children

Co-parenting can offer emotional stability to children following the separation or divorce of their parents. Regardless of the circumstances, a breakdown of the family structure can be traumatizing for a child. However, co-parenting can mitigate these effects by providing a consistent and loving environment where the child can express emotions and stay connected with both parents.

Children feel most secure when they have consistent contact with both parents who also actively cooperate and communicate with each other. This arrangement significantly reduces the tension and stress children might otherwise experience and encourages a greater sense of normalcy and stability in their lives.

Moreover, children witness their parents handling disputes amicably, demonstrating a model of conflict resolution that will be useful later in life.

7.3. Facilitating Resilience

Through co-parenting, children also learn resilience. It's a demonstration that the family can adapt and continue to function as a unit despite major life changes, such as divorce or separation. By working together and maintaining open lines of communication, the parents show the child that adversity can be overcome with effort and cooperation.

This is an invaluable lesson for children as they navigate future life challenges, and it can significantly enhance their resilience in the face of adversity.

7.4. Impact on Self-Esteem and Identity

A child's self-esteem and identity development also benefit greatly from co-parenting. When both parents, despite their differences, express unconditional love and maintain active involvement in the child's life, the child feels valued and important.

Children who feel loved and cherished by both parents are likely to develop a positive sense of self-worth, leading to improved self-esteem and a healthier identity formation.

7.5. Lessons on Relationships and Respect

Through effective co-parenting, children learn about mutual respect, reconciliation, empathy, and maintaining healthy relationships. They witness how adults manage differences, work together despite disagreements, and focus on common objectives, setting a powerful example for them.

These lessons lay the groundwork for their future interpersonal relationships and can help them cultivate meaningful, respectful bonds with others.

In essence, a well-executed co-parenting strategy can significantly influence a child's psychological development, providing them with emotional stability, teaching resilience, boosting self-esteem, and offering valuable lessons on relationships. However, it's crucial to remember that the success of co-parenting lies in the parents' willingness to work together and prioritize their child's wellbeing above anything else.

Chapter 8. Financial Aspects in Co-Parenting

Financial matters are among the most prickly to address when it comes to co-parenting, necessitating transparency, trust, and compromise.

8.1. Creating a Shared Budget

Shared parenting means sharing expenses, too. Both parties need to understand what it takes to maintain two homes for their children. A co-parenting budget is perhaps the most critical toolkit both parents need to have. Here's how you go about it:

Split these costs fairly. It's essential that both parents feel the arrangement is just and sustainable. A 50-50 split may seem fair, but if one parent earns significantly more than the other, you may choose to proportion expenses based on income.

Creating a shared budget is a crucial first step. This initial negotiation sets a precedent for later financial discussions. Remember, it's not just about fairness, but also openness and compromise.

8.2. Implementing the Shared Budget

Now that you've charted out a shared budget, you need to devise a system to implement it. There are various ways to do this, and you should choose an approach based on your comfort levels and relationship dynamics.

Physical or digital folders help keep track of expenses. Receipts and bills could be stored here as references for future discussions or disputes.

Regardless of the method chosen, regular reassessment of these decisions is crucial. As needs, income levels, and circumstances change, adjustments to the shared budget may be needed.

8.3. Child Support

A crucial factor in your financial planning is child support. This is an arrangement where one parent makes payments to the other for the upkeep of the child(ren). The parent who has the children less frequently typically pays the other parent.

Child support is often ordered by a court, based on a calculation that factors in the parents' income, time spent with the child, and the costs of childcare. If both parents share equal time, the higher earner may still be obliged to pay child support.

Naturally, this can be a contentious issue and it's better to reach an amicable agreement if possible. Consider child support as a method to provide your child with a standard of living that he or she would have enjoyed if the family had remained intact.

It's also important to be aware that child support payments typically cover only the necessities - food, shelter, and clothing. Costs related to education, healthcare, activities, and other special needs usually need to be negotiated separately.

8.4. College Savings

College expenses can be a significant financial challenge. As such, it's advisable to discuss and plan for them as soon as possible.

You may consider setting up a college savings account in your child's name. Sometimes, these savings can also be used for private elementary or secondary school tuition fees.

Both parents can make contributions to this account, and any support from grandparents or other relatives can also be deposited here. Agreement on the amount and frequency of these deposits is vital.

8.5. Maintaining Financial Stability

Shared parenting comes with its own set of responsibilities, and financial stability is critical. Ensuring you manage your finances well will go a long way in ensuring you can provide for your child and fulfill your responsibilities as a parent.

You may need to rethink your lifestyle and cut back on certain expenses to prioritize child-related costs. Regular saving is also essential. While a shared budget aids in managing joint expenses, you'll still need to manage your personal finances.

8.6. Navigating Financial dispute

Disagreements over financial issues can arise even with the best intentions and planning. In case of disagreement, refer back to your listed, agreed upon expenses, and your shared budget. Use these as guiding principles to reach a resolution.

Remember, the key to successful co-parenting is understanding, compromise, and focusing on what is best for the child. By managing financial aspects wisely, you can minimize conflicts, support each other's contributions, and provide your kids with the security they need to thrive.

Chapter 9. Maintaining Consistent Parenting Styles

One of the biggest challenges that co-parents face is the challenge of maintaining consistency in their parenting styles. A lack of consistency can result in confusion, frustration, and often, behavioral issues in children. As much as possible, it is crucial that both parents work together to establish and maintain a consistent set of rules, expectations, and consequences.

9.1. Understanding Parenting Styles

Every parent has their own parenting style that is influenced by their individual beliefs, values, and experiences. The four commonly recognized parenting styles are:

1. Authoritative: Authoritative parents set high standards and rules but are also warm and responsive to their children's needs. They encourage independence but also maintain control through clear, set boundaries.

2. Authoritarian: Authoritarian parents also set high standards and rules but are generally less responsive to their children's needs. They value obedience and discipline above all else.

3. Permissive: Permissive parents are warm and responsive but set few rules or standards. They tend to avoid confrontation and are more like friends to their children than authority figures.

4. Uninvolved: Uninvolved parents provide for their children's basic needs but are generally unresponsive and uninvolved in their lives.

Understanding your own parenting style and that of your co-parent is the first step to creating consistency. Once identified, you can begin to understand where potential conflicts may arise and develop strategies to mitigate them.

9.2. Creating a Unified Parenting Plan

Start by creating a unified parenting plan. This plan should detail all the aspects of children's upbringing that are important to both of you. Discuss everything from bedtimes to chores, homework, discipline, rewards, and even diet.

Here is a sample of what the parenting plan might look like in asciidoc syntax:

Issue	Your Plan	Co-parent's Plan	Agreed Plan
Bedtime	8:00 pm	9:00 pm	8:30 pm
Homework	After dinner	After school	After dinner
Sweets	Only on weekends	Everyday	Limited to once per day
Screen Time	One hour on weekdays	Unlimited	Two hours on weekdays

Compromise will be necessary for issues where there is a significant divide. The goal here is to find a middle ground that satisfies both parties while providing continuity for the kids.

9.3. Communication is Key

Communication is critical in creating and maintaining consistency. Regularly check-in with your co-parent about how things are going. Are the agreed rules being followed? Are they working? Do they need to be adjusted?

Use the following checklist as a guide for your discussions:

1. Are we both sticking to the agreed plan?

2. Are the children confused or upset by any aspects of the plan?

3. Are the rules working in both households?

4. Are there any new challenges or issues that need to be addressed?

5. Do we need to update the plan?

9.4. Addressing Differences and Disagreements

Despite your best efforts, disagreements and differences will inevitably arise. When they do, it is essential to handle them respectfully and constructively. Here are some strategies:

1. Choose a neutral time and place to discuss the disagreement.

2. Focus on the issue at hand — not on your ex-partner's character or past actions.

3. Listen to your co-parent's side of the story.

4. Respect their feelings and perceptions.

5. Seek a solution that is in your child's best interest.

9.5. Managing Transitions Between Households

Transitions between households can be a challenging time for children, especially when rules and expectations differ in both places. Here are some strategies to ease transition:

1. Establish and maintain a consistent schedule for transitions.

2. Keep a checklist of items that need to go with the child, such as school work or clothes.

3. Be positive and reassuring about transitions.

4. Have open communication about any issues that arise during transition periods.

In conclusion, maintaining consistent parenting styles in a co-parenting relationship is challenging but doable. It requires clear communication, respect, compromise, and a shared dedication to the well-being of your child. As co-parents, always keep in mind that your actions and decisions contribute significantly to your child's overall well-being and development. So make consistency a priority, for the sake of your child.

Chapter 10. Dealing with Conflict: Mature Approaches

Conflict is an unavoidable part of shared parenting, but how we manage it often creates the difference between a harmonious co-parenting relationship and a tumultuous one. In the heart of this challenge, stand maturity, compromise, and a shared commitment to the well-being of the children at stake.

10.1. Building a Collaborative Mindset

Developing a collaborative mindset forms the cornerstone of dealing with conflicts in shared parenting. A conflict is natural and inevitable whenever there are different perspectives, but when we learn to view it as an opportunity for negotiation and mutual understanding, we pave the way for mature handling of disagreements. This shift necessitates putting personal hearings aside and keeping our children's best interests at heart.

10.2. Communicating Effectively

Effective communication helps reduce conflict. This involves expressing your own needs and understanding the sentiments of your co-parent. Enlighten the other party about your concerns without accusing or blaming them. Unambiguous, honest communication fosters understanding and reduces erroneous assumptions - the root cause of many disagreements.

In an era where technology provides several mediums for communication, explore what works best for both parties. This could mean exchanging emails, using a shared calendar, or using co-parenting apps.

10.3. Cultivating Empathy

Empathy facilitates understanding, creates a conducive space for dialogue, and favors resolution. Seeing things from your co-parent's perspective minimizes resentment and fosters a mutual respect essential for successful conflict resolution.

10.4. Fostering Mutual Respect

Children mirror the behavior of their adults. Thus, maintaining mutual respect with your co-parent not only aids conflict resolution but also models healthy relationships for your children. Avoiding offensive language, respecting each other's time, and valuing the other parent's input are mandatory to cultivate respect in co-parenting relationships.

10.5. Developing a Conflict Resolution Strategy

Having a strategy for conflict resolution provides a roadmap to navigate through disagreements. It could involve identifying common triggers, acknowledging each other's emotions, brainstorming solutions, and reaching an agreement. Formalizing this strategy helps maintain an objective viewpoint, reducing emotional decisions.

10.6. Engaging in Mediation

Sometimes, despite the best intentions, conflicts might spiral out of control. In such instances, engaging a professional mediator proves beneficial. This neutral third party helps facilitate conversation and guide you towards coming to an amicable agreement.

10.7. Attending to Your Own Emotional Health

The emotional turmoil associated with shared parenting can often become overwhelming. Make sure to care for your emotional health to maintain a balanced perspective. This could include therapy, practicing mindfulness, or maintaining a support network of friends and family.

In conclusion, handling conflict in a mature manner involves developing a repertoire of strategies, including robust communication, mutual respect, empathy, and a robust conflict resolution strategy. Also crucial is the engagement of external resources when necessary and prioritizing your own emotional health. By imbibing these strategies, you can transform conflicts into opportunities for growth, fostering a nurturing environment for your children.

Chapter 11. Co-Parenting Success Stories: Lessons from Real Life

Navigating the world of co-parenting can be challenging, so having some successful examples to learn from can make all the difference. In this section, we delve into real stories of co-parenting success and distill the valuable lessons each offers.

11.1. From Enemies to Allies

Joan and Alex, parents to vibrant twins, divorced when their children were just toddlers. Initially, the relationship was caustic; both despised each other and every pick-up and drop-off was a battlefield. They knew something had to change for their children's wellbeing so they sought counseling. They underwent joint therapy sessions to work on their issues and learned how to communicate effectively.

Lesson: The couple learned the importance of communication. Even if the relationship started rocky, effective and open communication can turn things around. This included discussing schedules in advance, expressing concerns clearly, and being open about changes. Communication became their steering wheel in navigating their new co-parenting journey.

11.2. Overcoming Business of Life

Sarah and Mark were both career-oriented people with busy schedules. Post-divorce, they found it challenging to manage their parental duties amidst their professional responsibilities. But they soon created a shared calendar system. Every detail related to their daughter Lucy's school functions, doctors' appointments, or any unexpected event is added to this digital calendar, set with reminders.

Lesson: Organization is key in managing shared responsibilities. Technology can play a significant role in achieving this. Shared calendars, note apps, and other online tools can streamline co-parenting tasks and reduce the chance of misunderstandings or forgotten commitments.

11.3. Accepting New Challenges

Patricia and Steven had an amicable divorce but ran into trouble when Patricia started dating. Initially, Steven found it difficult to accept a new man's role in his children's lives. After a few months, however, he realized the positive influence Patricia's partner had on the kids.

Lesson: Accepting new partners can be a challenge in co-parenting. However, it's important to look at the bigger picture: how is this affecting the children? Putting feelings of jealousy or discomfort aside and prioritizing children's needs is vital.

11.4. Understanding Children's Needs

Post-divorce, David and Mary agreed on a shared parenting plan. Still, their son Andy was not adapting well. Both parents noticed he was stressed. They decided to involve a child psychologist, who suggested tweaking their parenting plan to give Andy a more stable routine.

Lesson: A child's needs should take precedence in any co-parenting arrangement. These needs might change over time or may not even align with your initial parenting plan. Being willing to adapt for your child's wellbeing is paramount in successful co-parenting.

11.5. The Power of Consistency

Mike and Anna divorced when their daughter was 10 years old. Despite their differences, they agreed to keep rules and disciplinary techniques consistent across both households. This consistency made transitions between homes smoother for their child, and it clarified expectations.

Lesson: Consistency in parenting styles, rules, and routines across households can help children adjust better to the new family dynamics. It ensures a sense of familiarity and security for the child, no matter which parent they are with.

In summary, successful co-parenting encompasses elements of open communication, organization, acceptance of new partners, the ability to adapt to children's needs, and a commitment to consistent parenting. Regardless of personal differences, parents united by the common aim of their child's best interest can create a nurturing and balanced environment for their children. It requires dedication, compromise, and an immense amount of care, but the payoff – seeing your children thrive, is worthwhile.

www.ingramcontent.com/pod-product-compliance
Lightning Source LLC
Chambersburg PA
CBHW071003250726
48663CB00002B/359